THIS
COWORKER
HAS 101 PROBLEMS
BUT
COLORING AIN'T ONE

Our passion is creating unique, funny and affordable coloring gifts.

Gracewinterbooks

Grace Winter - Coloring Books

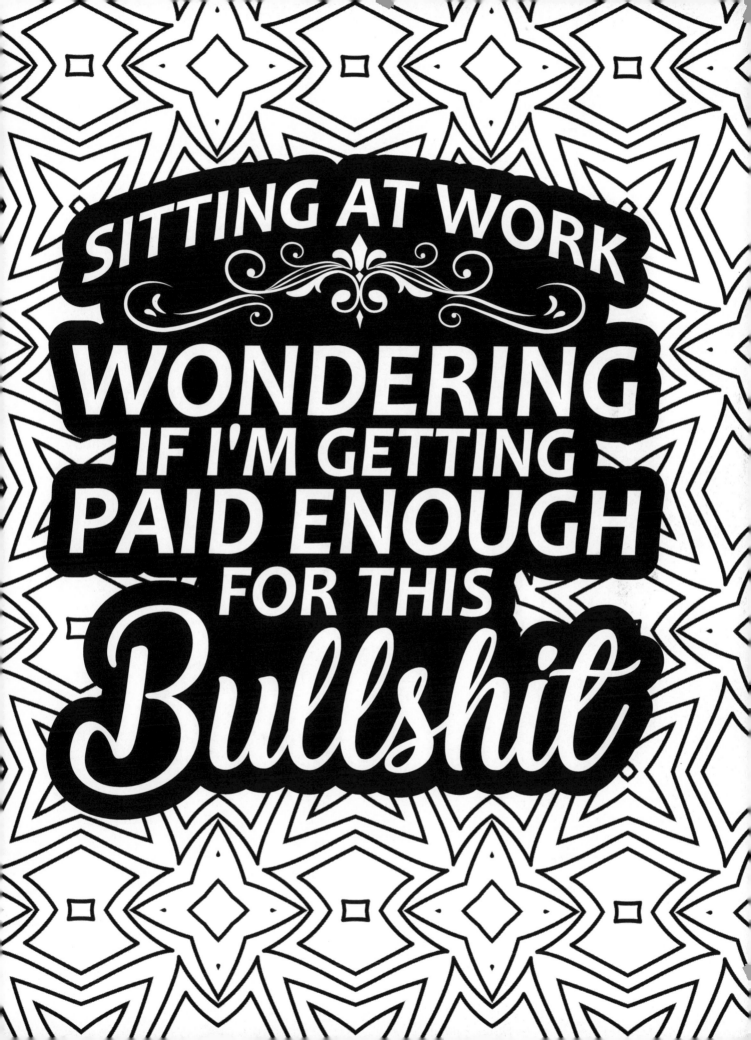

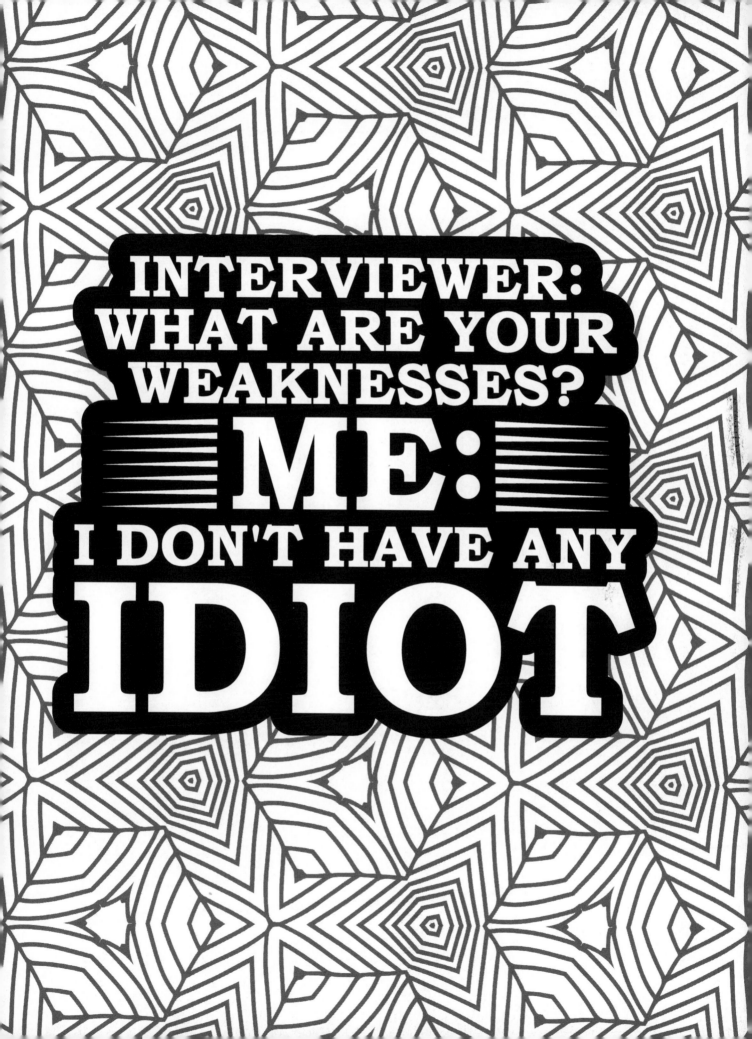

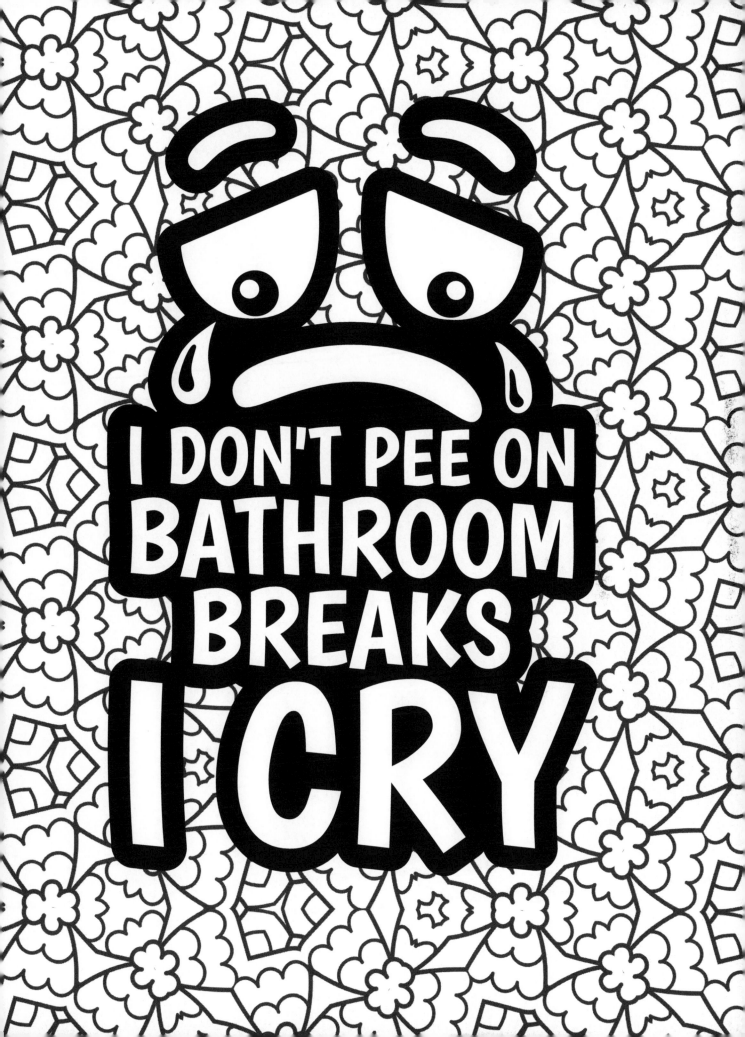

"It's been a long week" ME IN THE MIDDLE OF TUESDAY

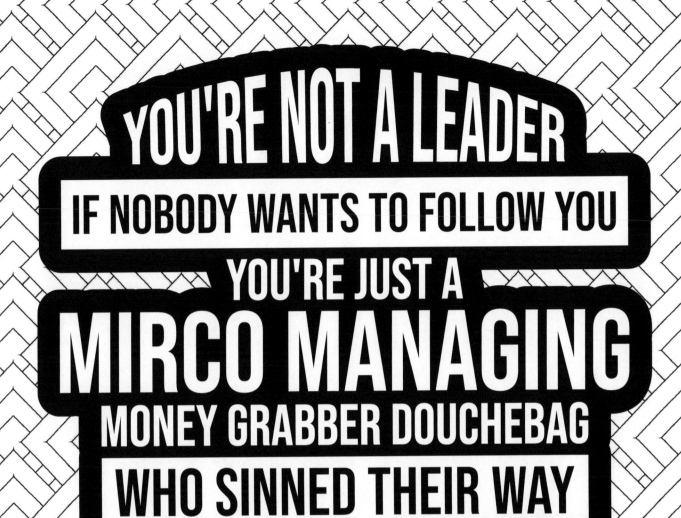

YOU'RE NOT A LEADER
IF NOBODY WANTS TO FOLLOW YOU
YOU'RE JUST A
MIRCO MANAGING
MONEY GRABBER DOUCHEBAG
WHO SINNED THEIR WAY
INTO BEING IN CHARGE

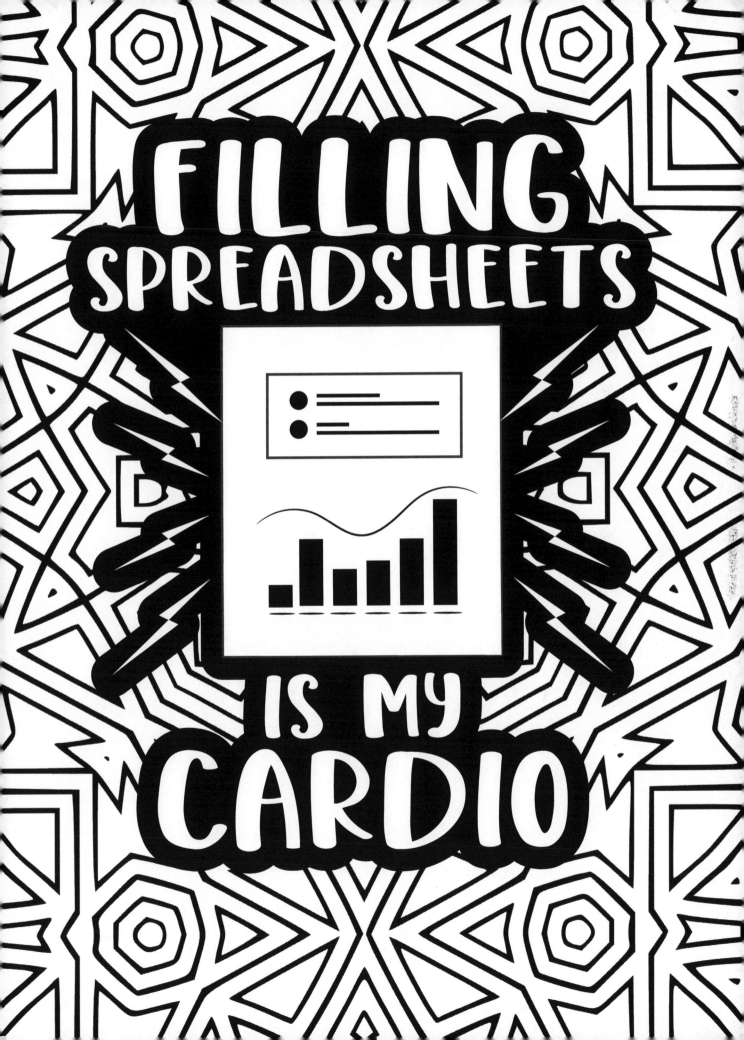

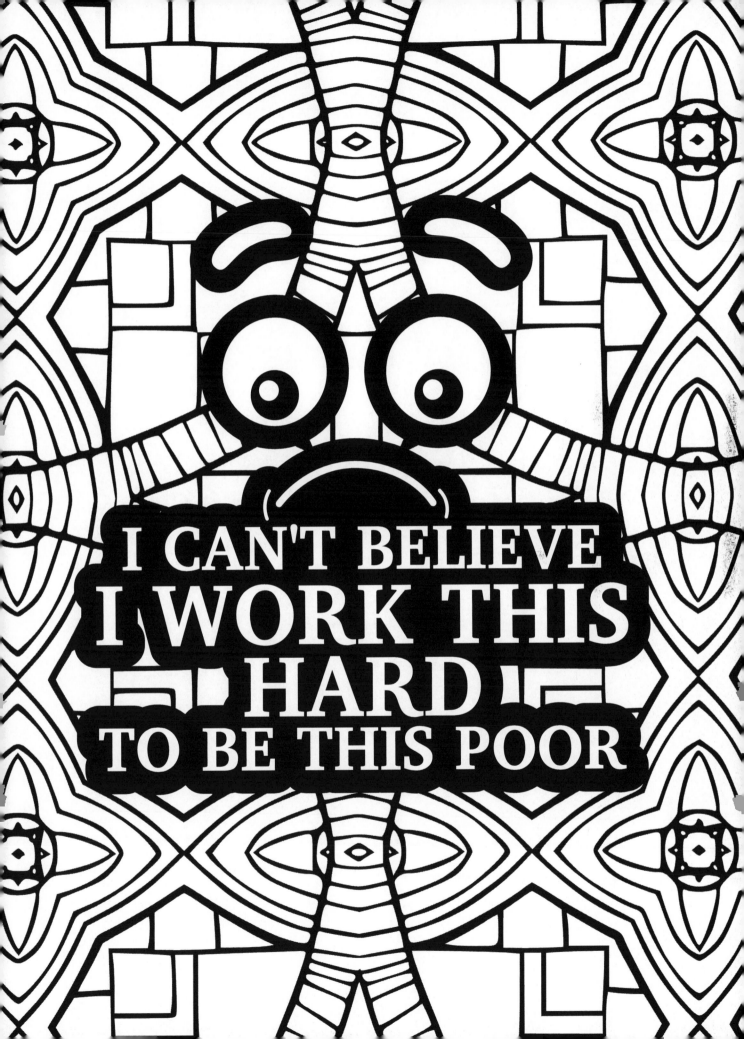

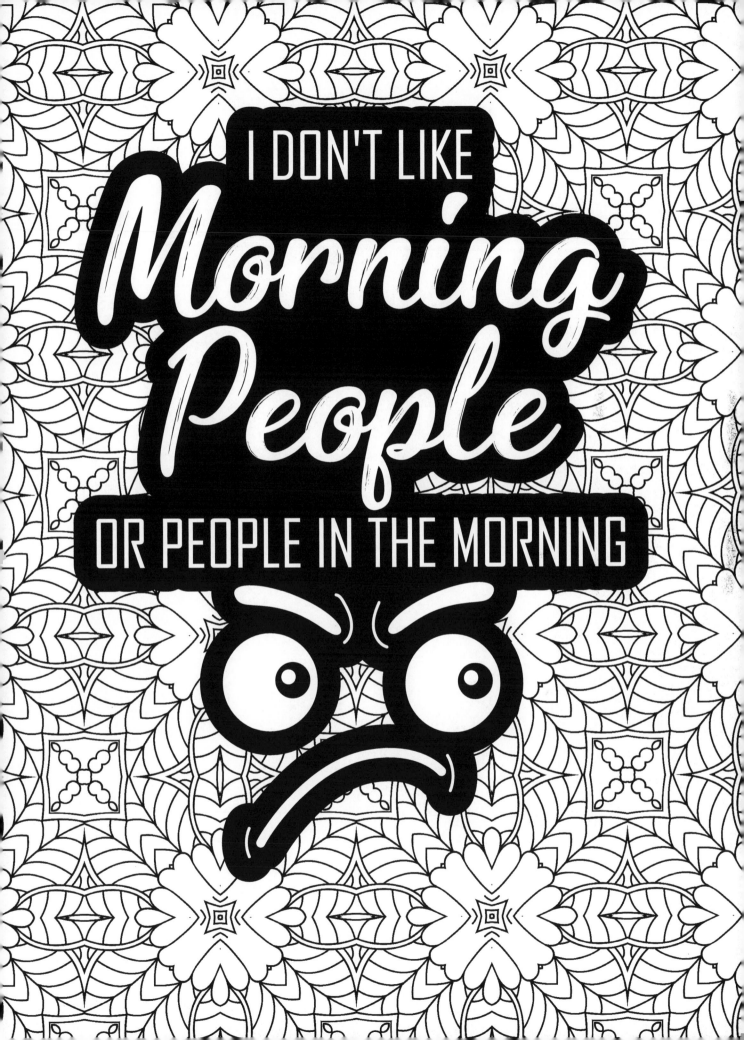

Our passion is creating unique, funny and affordable coloring gifts.

Printed in Great Britain
by Amazon